Make Believe

Make Believe

Poems for Hoping Again

Victoria Hutchins

CONVERGENT

NEW YORK

Published in the United States by Convergent Books, an imprint of Random House, a division of Penguin Random House LLC, New York.

CONVERGENT BOOKS is a registered trademark and the Convergent colophon is a trademark of Penguin Random House LLC.

Grateful acknowledgment is made to The Charlotte Sheedy Literary Agency for permission to reprint four lines from "Sometimes" from *Red Bird* by Mary Oliver, copyright © 2008, 2017 by Mary Oliver. Reprinted by permission of The Charlotte Sheedy Literary Agency as agent for the author and Bill Reichblum.

LIBRARY OF CONGRESS CATALOGING-IN-PUBLICATION DATA
Names: Hutchins, Victoria, author.
Title: Make believe / by Victoria Hutchins.
Description: New York, NY: Convergent, [2025] |
"A Convergent Books Trade Paperback Original."
Identifiers: LCCN 2024041006 (print) | LCCN 2024041007 (ebook) |
ISBN 9780593735718 (paperback) | ISBN 9780593735725 (ebook)
Subjects: LCSH: Wonder—Poetry. | Joy—Poetry. | Hope—Poetry. |
LCGFT: Poetry.
Classification: LCC PS3608.U85925 M35 2025 (print) |
LCC PS3608.U85925 (ebook) | DDC 811/.6—dc23/eng/20240911
LC record available at https://lccn.loc.gov/2024041006
LC ebook record available at https://lccn.loc.gov/2024041007

Printed in the United States of America on acid-free paper

convergentbooks.com

1st Printing

For the child you are at heart,
who still believes in magic.

Only if there are angels in your head will you
ever, possibly, see one.

—Mary Oliver

contents

II. A World Where Your Body Feels like Home

III. A World Where Hope Grows Back

IV. A World Where Love Calls the Shots

V. A World Where Heaven Happens Now

Make Believe

how to play make believe

To start, befriend eight-year-old you. Tell them they were right about everything. Together, build a castle using only a bedsheet. Close your eyes and listen for your grandpa's voice in the wind. Run into the forest like it's a portal to another world. Have a tea party with stuffed animal guests and go on and on about how the plastic food is delicious. Notice when you start to believe it.

Resolve to have faith in the rosy and impractical. Decide all dogs go to heaven and imaginary friends are real. Write a story where things work out in the end. Jump off the high dive even if you tremble climbing the ladder. Pay no mind to how your body looks doing it. Dig out your costume box and try on different versions of yourself. Make a pinky promise to stay friends forever and try to actually keep it. Turn off your phone and lie in a garden. Pray to anything that feels holy. Notice how everything feels holy when you pay attention. Open the door when pain knocks, but leave the porch light on for joy. Choose to trust that it will get better and tell yourself the good news every morning.

Maybe you're not old enough yet to believe in fairy tales again. But you can take a walk with optimism. You can hear her out when she tells you the universe is conspiring in your favor, and keep your eyes peeled for signs that she's right. The wishes and the miracles and the magic can help, but you don't need them. It will be you, deciding your life deserves hope. Making a life worth believing in.

I.

A World of Reclaimed Wonder

A woman will return,
looking for the girl she was.

—Louise Glück

welcome to the world

Welcome to the world. You're going to get hurt here. Your friend will tell you she's staying in and then you'll see a picture of her at the mall with your other friends. You'll get strep throat every winter. You'll get a new shirt that you love. Then, you'll get teased about it at school and change into your gym clothes for the rest of the day. A stranger will drag their car key across the paint of your mom's new car that made the whole family proud. A giant pimple will sprout on the tip of your nose the day before prom. You'll say something hateful to your sister and learn that the worst punishment is the hurt you see on her face. One Tuesday, the person who held your hand on the bus for three months will wordlessly sit with someone else. And if I'm honest, that's just the beginning.

But—has anyone told you about fireflies? And have you been to the beach? Have you looked at a leaf closely enough to notice its veins—closely enough to understand it's the same thing as you? Have you had a McDonald's Coke? And did you know that in the three seconds before you kiss someone for the first time, you can feel your heartbeat in your eyelids? Or that someday, when you finally tell someone about the thing you're sure makes you irredeemable, and you search their eyes for disgust—you'll find only love?

Welcome to the world. You're going to get hurt here, and then you'll beg for seconds:

Can I have just a few more seconds?

see the light

Peer in any window and you'll find light and dark, head to head.
Your neighbor's dad dropped dead: a hemorrhagic stroke. That
night, her fourteen-year-old son clung to her for the first time
in three years. Your cousin got robbed at an ATM. The robber
used the cash to buy a crib and that was the last night his baby
had to sleep in the top drawer. Your sister got bullied so badly
she had to transfer to a new school. She met her future wife on
the first day there. The family dog got inoperable cancer. On her
way to her euthanasia appointment, her belly was covered in
park mud and she wagged her tail for the first time in months.

An old woman just died alone in the hospital. Two floors up,
fresh life is kicking and screaming its way into the arena, wails
piercing the morning.

Hideous odds and yet, a battle cry.

primordial rage
in a pink blanket

When my clock started, the ticking sound enraged me.
Mortality is loud when you were infinite just a moment ago.

I tried to tell the others. I would scream till I passed out, then
sputter awake and start again. When my mother left the room,
I erupted. I didn't have the words to say: *Please come back.*
We don't have much time together—I can hear the moments
passing.

go seek

You're six.
You wake up from a bad dream
and run to your parents' room to ask if it was real.
No, baby, it isn't real. It was just a dream.
Somewhere in the universe, all the bad things
are still just dreams.

You're seven.
You're on the playground playing hide-and-go-seek.
You're shouting, *I'll be the seeker!*
Somewhere in the universe, it still hasn't occurred to you
to hide.

You're eight.
It's bedtime and you're fighting it.
Can I have five more minutes? One more minute?
Somewhere in the universe, time is still worth
begging for.

fortune teller

My friends and I are playing games at lunch.
We fold a sheet of paper until it tells us our future,
then smooth it out and write M.A.S.H. at the top.

We're all anticipation and knobby knees,
jumper pockets full of jingling days to come.
We know exactly how we want to spend them,
but if we get stuck, we just pick a color
and a number and let our fate flow
from our best friend's fingers to God's ears.

Will you live in a mansion, apartment,
shack, or house? Who will you marry?
What will your job be? How many kids?

We are blank sheets and these are simple questions,
with simple answers. We haven't thought to doubt
whether our lives will turn out fine, so we just
play for fun.

you used to ask why

Why you weren't allowed
to play outside by yourself.
Why you had to call home when
you made it to your friend's house.
Why you needed to ask before
you went anywhere with anybody,
even into another room.
Why, why, why, you asked,
in the blessed before.

Until one day, you were tall enough
to see it for yourself: the field of danger
and stories and reasons beyond the gate.
The sign at its entrance: *BECAUSE I SAID SO.*

judgment day

I'm seven years old and I can't stop ruining things. Yesterday
I broke my mom's herringbone necklace. The day before that,
it was the buckle of her pocketbook. And today, my juice
spilled on the new bedding.

As always, I am very sorry. I tremble over to my mom, clutching
the evidence, and show her what I did. She is not happy, but
she is not mad. She pulls me into her lap and wipes my tears
and together we inspect the damage.

If there's a reckoning after this life for the mistakes we made
in it, I hope it's something like this. I hope the universe pulls
me into her lap and combs her fingers through my hair while I
tell her what I did. I hope she says, *Oh honey, I know you didn't
mean to. Of course I still love you. Yes, I think we can fix it.
I think it will all come out in the wash.*

the swing of things

Do you remember the first time you pumped your legs
for dear life, and jumped? How the chains went slack
as you hurled yourself out of the mildewed canvas seat?
How, for that one airborne second, nothing else mattered?

When was the last time you were alone with your heartbeat
and the sky?

When did you forget how to let go?

church hath no wisdom
like a child wondering

On the first day of vacation bible school,
us kids spotted cockroaches in the chapel.
The next morning, the church administrator
assured each adult in the drop-off line
that an exterminator was on the case.
One little girl asked what an exterminator was
and was told. She frowned and said:
What if the cockroaches just wanted
to go to vacation bible school like me?

God, grant me the sageness of a child.
Help me remember how to look at what
I'm told is a disposable life
and see my own face.
God, restore the boundlessness of the cup
of that which I deem like me,
like you.

sugarcoat

Little sister: one part pest and one part pining.
You say you aren't copying, but you are.
You don't want to wear a jacket.
You don't want to be eight.
You want to play with the big girls.
You want to be twelve, just like them.

Today, when I heard about the Allen outlet mall shooting,
the first thing I thought about was you. You,
furious that you weren't allowed to walk our mall alone.
Mortified by the notion of needing to be protected.

I am begging you: Let eight be eight. Let twelve be twelve.
Let bigger hands guide your arms through your sleeves.
Someday the bitter cold will come, and you will understand
why your sugarcoat was zipped up to the neck.

come out, come out,
wherever you are

It's a midnight in fifth grade and there's a monster in the closet.
It hides behind your winter coats and pom-poms. You're too
scared to get up to turn on the light. What if it leaps out of the
closet, or worse: pulls you in? Someday when you're older, you
won't be afraid of the monster. You can't see it from where
you are now, but all along, it was a shadow.

It's a midnight in college and there's a secret in the closet.
It hides behind your overzealous allyship and verses from
Leviticus. You're too scared to get drunk with your friends.
What if you tell the truth, or worse: act on it? Someday
when you're older, you won't be afraid of the secret. You
can't see it from where you are now, but all along, it was
a blessing.

supernatural

The night of my sleepover birthday party, my mom had my aunt Julia prank-call the house. Aunt Julia breathed heavily into the phone and every girl at the party shrieked. I was half convinced a ghost was on the other end of the line and half playing along for the thrill of it.

Next, we played *light as a feather, stiff as a board*. I lay on my back while the other girls scooted their palms under me and lifted me up. Then, they each tried to pull one hand away while they chanted:

Light as a feather, stiff as a board
Light as a feather, stiff as a board
Light as a feather, stiff as a board

The idea is that the chant summons a supernatural force that lightens the load. (Anyone who has played the game knows it does not.)

It's fun to pretend. Maybe there's no such thing as ghosts, god, or lucky stars. Maybe everything I have ever attributed to otherworldly forces is the work of human hands. So what? I'll take every drop of natural magic I can get. If the closest thing to a god this life has to offer is my mom, my aunt Julia, and the hands of my friends, fine by me.

I'd pray to that any day.

god as imaginary friend

You're too old to have imaginary friends,
the kids on the school bus once said.
I waited till they weren't looking and turned to her.
Don't listen to them. You're real to me.
You're the only one who hasn't left and if you're not real,
I don't want to know.

You're too smart to believe in God,
the man on the picnic blanket with me said.
I looked away from my date and turned to god.
Don't listen to him. You're real to me.
You're the only one who hasn't left and if you're not real,
I don't want to know.

That's the thing about imaginary friends.
If you never stop believing in them, they're just friends.

fitting room

Do you remember in college when we went
to the Goodwill on 88th to get out of the rain?
When you tried on the assless chaps with the church hat
and I tried on the green velvet tuxedo and we laughed
and laughed, asking each other, *Could this be the new me?*

What do you say we go try on some other versions of ourselves?
Let's dress up in every style they have on the racks. I'll help you
with the buttons on your most impractical dream. Swing the
fitting room door open again and again. *Does this look good on
me? Could I make this fit? Could this be the new me?*

Yes, yes, yes.

it's not too late

To glue purple rhinestones to your phone. Throw yourself a
Totally Spies! birthday party. Drink apple juice from a teacup.
Build a sandcastle. Eat Lucky Charms. Dress up as the red
Power Ranger. Get a hamster. Camp out on a trampoline. Wear
a candy necklace. Make a friendship bracelet. Ride a dirt bike.
Run in the sprinkler. Pitch a tent in the yard. Crimp your hair.
Graduate. Get a tattoo. Post on the Internet. Start dressing
masculine or feminine. Throw those words in the trash. Start
questioning. Stop questioning. Throw caution to the wind.
Hold hands with the younger versions of yourself that live
inside of you. Create a new version.

When I was twenty-five, I wanted to sign up for dance lessons,
but I thought I was too old. That it was too late. If I could go
back in time, I would shake my shoulders and say, *Listen to
me—we are only here for a second. You will be young for every
moment of your life, and then you will be gone. Don't waste
another second of the music wondering if it's too late to dance.*

birthday cake recipe
(feeds none)

1 cup secret expectations, unmet
12 ounces existential dread, thawed
3 teaspoons of I'm not a child anymore and I never will be again
1 package of I know we're not official but I thought they'd do
        something (store-bought is fine)
1 heaping tablespoon of not where I thought I'd be at this age
        (or more to taste)
4 eggs (fertile if you have them)
3 scoops of I remembered theirs but they didn't remember mine
1 ripe realization that your mother had been married for eight
        years at this age
1 year closer to dying
1 14-ounce can of holy shit (I am going to die flavor)
2 friends who remembered
4 cups of will I be remembered?

Blend until teary. Bake at 350°F for 18–20 minutes.
Yield: One happy birthday. (Happiness not included.)

is the party dead already?

If you've always been on the outside looking in,
when you're finally invited to the party,
you might find that up close,
the life of it has hollow eyes.
And the glass house you looked into longingly
was rose-colored all along.

II.

A World Where Your Body Feels like Home

The most beautiful part of your body
is where it's headed.

—Ocean Vuong

unbiting the apple

You know how when Eve bit the apple, she suddenly became aware she was naked and felt ashamed? What was your biting-the-apple moment? The moment when you were taught your body is something to be ashamed of? When you were little, your body was just your vessel. You wolfed down ice creams at the pool, unashamed of your hunger. Unaware that your belly poked out when you finished. The shape of your stomach, the hair on your legs, and the bump on your nose were all just flowers in your Garden of Eden. It never would have occurred to you to scrutinize them.

Until one day, someone squinted at your flowers and said, *That one is really big.* And just like that, the bitten apple fell from your hand. The tree of knowledge started shouting. And you suddenly noticed—it *was* really big.

You cannot unbite the apple. But tonight you are alone with your flowers. And this garden of blood and breath and flesh belongs to you alone. You cannot unsee, unhear, unknow. But you can kiss each flower in your garden on the forehead. You can plant new ones and protect them with everything you have. You can close the garden gates. You can ask God if she'll take the first watch.

how to become unrecognizable by summer

Water with lemon, hot.
No gluten.
No GMOs.
No processed foods.
No added sugar.
No eating until noon.
Ten percent incline, forty-five minutes. No days off.
Remember that fruit carbs are still carbs.

Let some time pass.

You used to write poetry before bed but lately you can't hold
your eyes open. You used to love to bake but now it's *too
tempting*. You used to love stopping for a doughnut on the way
home from the dog park, carefully picking out a Boston cream
and a maple bar, but now when your boyfriend asks, you say,
No, I'm trying to be good. You used to listen when your friends
talked, but tonight you can't stop looking at the bread on the
table. You add up what you've eaten today, say to yourself,
Okay, one piece, no butter, and I'll go for a run after this.
First thing in the morning, you used to pray. Now you
go straight to the bathroom mirror, pull up your shirt,
and look at your stomach.

Congratulations! You don't recognize yourself.

while the getting is good

Once when my mother was in second grade, she was drinking
the last bit of a glass of milk, slurping away through a straw.
Her teacher asked her, *Do you know what that sound is for?*
She said she didn't. He replied, *It lets a fool know he's
reached the bottom of the glass.*

Trust me, I know my drink (my time, my youth, your attention)
is dwindling. But I want the last drop, and how else will I get it?

Sure, I would love for my wanting to be less obvious.
But I came into the world hungry, and I intend to leave licking
the plate. I came into the world thirsty, and I'll slurp until
the glass is taken away.

know no master

Imagine an alternate universe where *diet* isn't in the dictionary. A world where the magazine covers read *HUMAN STEM CELL BREAKTHROUGH* and *DAWN SPACECRAFT LAUNCHED* instead of *JUMBO JESSICA SIMPSON* and *STARS LOSE FIGHT WITH CELLULITE*. Where you don't know the StairMaster from Adam. There, you didn't spend your second year of law school eating half a sweet potato for lunch, so you know more about family law and less about how to stop yourself from fainting mid-faint.

Imagine all the extra room in your mind. The reclaimed time in a day. You learn Italian for the hell of it. You bike to the beach every Sunday just to eat fried fish on a thick-aired patio and let the hills remind your lungs that they're alive. You learn how to play the flute. You know the song of every bird in your state by heart. They all sound so natural, like how it's supposed to be.

shapeshifter

Did you know there are seven species that change color
better than chameleons? Cuttlefish, several types of octopus,
and the golden tortoise beetle. But the star of the show is me.

I don't know how to stop turning myself into the shade of
woman that matches the room. I'm shy if you're funny. I'm
funny if you're shy. My voice flies high if I want you to think
I'm sweet, and low if I want you to think I'm smart. I'm like
a snake that drags all my old skins behind me, in case
someone thinks one of them suits me better.

Sometimes in the moments before they die, chameleons erupt
with color. Blues, greens, reds, the bright yellow of the sun.
Everything all at once. Maybe when my life flashes before my
eyes at the end of all this, I'll see every shade of woman I ever
was. Maybe on the other side waits my nature before nurture.
Some iridescent, steady thing.

what peace weighs

Tell me about the weight you gained this summer.

The weight you gained slurping vodka Sprites at the gay bar
the last night before your friends left town. Melting into a sea
of glitter and leather, tipping your head back to get every drop.

The weight you gained soaking biscuits with molasses and gravy
at your mom's kitchen table. Running your fingers over your
aunt's pink fingernails in between bites. Asking the name of
the color. Noticing how her fingers look just like your mom's.

The weight you gained gripping a burger on a picnic blanket
with the person you love. Wiping greasy fingers on the grass.
Remembering when you were too scared to really eat in front
of them. Feeding fries to the dog. Asking questions that used
to scare you but don't anymore: *What do you think is in
the secret sauce? Where do you see us in five years? Ten?*

The weight you gained celebrating pregnancies and promotions
and divorces. Squeezing red icing letters onto a grocery store
cake. Spelling out *SHE'S FREE.*

Tell me about the weight you gained this summer.
And then tell me—would you give it back if you could?

natural remedies

If you want to fix your stretch marks,
watch lightning stretch across the sky when it rains.
When you want to fix your crooked bottom teeth,
hike until you can see a jagged mountain range.
When you want to fix your acne scars,
run your hand across the bark of a tree.
When you want to fix your thigh fat,
dive into the rippled, massive sea.

When you feel an urge to fix your body,
cast yourself into the rough of this world.
Spend a day in her peaks and plains and valleys.
Run your hands through her sand, shells, and pearls.
Feel how hairy and bumpy and big she is.
Do you think that she needs to be fixed?

digital age whiplash

Celebrity and Other Celebrity spotted amid breakup rumors /
Deadly shooting at Georgia elementary school / Rams win
Super Bowl / Over 20 species declared extinct in 2023 /
Celebrity mocks Other Celebrity's eyebrows, sparking viral feud
/ Transgender violent deaths surge after anti-trans legislation /
Dow up 400 points / Over 20 million women below poverty line
/ UFC fight predictions: There will be blood / Drama at the Met
Gala / Air strike death toll exceeds 20,000 / Celebrity rescues cat
from tree: Faith in humanity restored / Dramatic eating
disorder spike for preteen girls / Celebrity pairs baby bump
with legs for miles / New study estimates 26,000 rape-related
pregnancies in Texas after outlawing abortion / Celebrity sizzles
in red / Climate change pace accelerates / New study shows
redwood trees are dying young / New study predicts childhood
depression will skyrocket in 2030 / New study asks: In the age of
information overload, how can we hold it all?

reconciliation story

Once upon a time, Brain met Body. Brain taught Body how to run and play. Body helped Brain play with toys. Brain reminded Body to eat breakfast. Body took Brain anywhere Brain wanted to go. They were best friends.

Time passed, and they grew up. Brain changed. Body changed too. When Body asked to eat breakfast with Brain like they used to, Brain got mad. Brain was never happy with Body, even when Body tried to do everything Brain asked. When they looked in the mirror, they saw different things. Body didn't feel good enough for Brain anymore, but Body didn't have anyone else but Brain. They both stuck around but stopped trusting each other, and eventually they grew apart.

Many years passed, and they grew older. Brain still wanted to run and play, but Body couldn't run anymore. Brain wanted to eat breakfast, but Body was too tired to come to the table. Brain missed Body, and realized the error of its ways. Brain said sorry. Body forgave.

For the first time in a long time, Body felt loved. So it mustered up a little energy and asked, *Brain, what can I do for you today?*

Brain said, *You've done enough, Body. Close your eyes. I'll take you anywhere you want to go.*

so relatable

I'm struck by how pain is the glue of womanhood.
We are never more likable than when we are failing.
We are never more relatable than when we are suffering.
User237837289238 said she used to think I was annoying
until I said the words *eating disorder*. Now, I'm an inspiration.

Sometimes I think I ham it up too much,
clarion-calling for connection:
Look at me, same type of sick as you.
Does your hurt look like mine?
Do you like me better for it?

I dream about the day when I'll write about joy,
about unbridled wellness of mind and spirit
and comment sections full of women will say,
Same. I feel this.
This is so real, so me, so relatable.
This is the story of my life.

the sun and sons

Here on Earth, we rise with the sun.
Here on Earth, we bend the knee to sons.

Here on Earth, a mother brushing her daughter's hair
is a mother brushing her daughter's hair
and a father brushing his daughter's hair
is a viral sensation, so wholesome it makes you cry.

Here on Earth, men get finer with age
and women who still think they're pretty at forty are *brave*.

Here on Earth, the sky is blue
except for every now and then—
when the atmosphere is dusty
(but not *too* dusty,
sexy but not *too* sexy,
smart but not *too* smart)—
the sky blooms pink.

Somewhere in the universe,
I hope there's a planet that rises with the moon.

Where the man creatures dumb themselves down
to make the woman creatures want them.

Where if a mother takes her child to the doctor,
the men at the front desk coo about how she's
So involved. What sweet bonding time.
Where a woman in the C-suite is an executive

and a man in the C-suite is a *#boyboss, you go, boy, lean in!*
Where 92 percent of global leaders are women
but lots of corporations are selling things
in the name of male empowerment
so they're *definitely* making progress.

Where the sky is pink most days
except for every now and then,
when the sky blooms blue.

On second thought, an eye for an eye
makes the whole world cry.
I don't want anyone to shrink so that I can feel tall.
What I really hope is that somewhere in the universe,
there's a planet beholden to nothing at all.
Where the creatures rise when they please,
and the sky is every color at the same time,
and gender is a silly human idea
that has never crossed their creature minds.

permission slip

to eat a corn dog during Whole30 / and quit 75 Hard on day 7 /
or day 1 / to get a full sleeve tattoo / even if it horrifies your
grandma / to pierce your nose / your eyebrow / your nipples /
to get a tooth gem / even if your boyfriend thinks they look like
cavities / to wear the skirt that makes your mom *not mad, just
disappointed* / to treat your body like it's yours / and your life
like it's yours / to snatch the book of permission slips / and
take off running down the hall

let her eat cake

Somewhere in the blanket of time,
Your future self is thinking of you.
She's eighty-nine.
Her wrinkled hands rest in her lap,
skin like butterfly wings,
veins like roots.

She watches as you open the fridge,
look at your leftover birthday cake,
and then close it.
I'm not hungry, you tell yourself.
I don't need it.

She's on her last few cakes.
Listen, as she licks her lips.

keep them on their toes

What type of woman will you be?
They need to know where to put you.
You and your lithe limbs, arched back,
firm handshake, ten-dollar word,
apple pie, cross necklace,
trying to have it all.

Go on, surrender to being sorted.
Put your best foot forward
and cross the other one behind it.
Hold your glass by the stem
and put your napkin in your lap.
Let out a tiny wind-chime giggle
whenever the men at the table laugh.

And once they decide
what type of *thing* you are,
once they crown you a good girl,
once they pat you on the head and tell you
Good women like you are hard to find,
pat your napkin to your mouth,
say, *If you'll kindly excuse me,*
then duck under the tablecloth, and bite
every ankle between you and the door.

my body is a temple

My body is a temple, but not the type I was taught.
There is no steeple, no solemn stained-glass faces,
no man at the pulpit. No pews with wooden pockets
full of commandments and songs I don't know.
My temple is a sprawling promise
with walls of flesh and bone and choice.
The bump on its nose, an altar to my grandmother.
Its scars, a shrine to myself.
Etched in the foundation are the words:
I was here, I was here, I was here,
the scrawl of every hand from my bloodline.

My body is a temple, and I will use my temple to worship.
I will make love. I will make time.
I will make promises and try to keep them.
I will make breakfast when I do not believe I deserve it.
I will fling open every window and shout about hope,
even when I don't feel it. Especially when I don't feel it.

My temple was not bought with blood. It is not for sale.
I will be here till it crumbles.
I will spend every second I am offered
in this sacred home
made for my holy spirit.

III.

A World Where Hope Grows Back

to love life, to love it even
when you have no stomach for it

—Ellen Bass

grounding exercise

The first few months of staying alive might feel like going through the world's dumbest motions. You'll try everything anyone says will help and maybe none of it will. You'll buy a gratitude journal and roll your eyes as you write down affirmations: *I want to be here. It will get better. I see the good in me.* You'll read the book that cured your neighbor's dad's depression and hate it. You'll have your coffee on the front porch instead of the couch every day in August and barely even notice you're outside. You'll clench your jaw through countless guided meditations, inhaling through your nose and exhaling to a silky disembodied voice's count of three. You'll tell the crisis hotline worker three things you can see, two things you can hear, and one thing you can feel—and all of it will be made up.

In the end, the only currency your pain will accept is time. Once you've paid the piper his days, any mundane thing might lift the fog—your sister's laugh, the sound of your dog's toenails on the hardwood, the same song you listen to every day. Slowly, your soul will blink its eyes open after a hibernation you would have sworn was a death.

And there it will be, just when you thought you were dead inside: one thing you can feel.

reasons to stick around
for a while

If it's spring, stick around for summer. Soon the sun will burn
off the clouds by 8 A.M. most days. You'll feel it on your
shoulders during your morning walks. You'll sit on yoga mats in
parks until the rubber burns your legs, laughing at stories
you've heard a hundred times. You'll run barefoot in wet grass.
You'll lie on a towel in your driveway and eat watermelon slices.
It will stay light outside until 9 P.M. You'll get a gas station
slushie and it will taste exactly like it did when you were a kid.
You'll go to the pool and see lots of bodies in bathing suits.
You'll remember that bodies don't look how they look on the
Internet. You'll swim in the ocean and think about how people
have brought their problems to it for millennia. You'll
remember you are part of something infinite.

If it's summer, stick around for fall. Soon there will be a chill in
the air when you leave for work. You'll go thrift-shopping for
sweaters. You'll sit on bleachers in a sea of tipsy people and
shout about what's happening on the field (even though you
don't understand what's happening on the field). You'll glue
rhinestones onto your Halloween costume all October. You'll
drink chai lattes. You'll watch scary movies and look away
during the scary parts and laugh at the jump scares. You'll go to
a haunted house and scream until you're hoarse. The leaves will
change colors and then fall to the ground. You'll remember
change and loss are natural. You'll burn your casserole and
everyone at Friendsgiving will eat it anyway. You'll remember
there are people who will take you whole, burnt parts and all.

If it's fall, stick around for winter. Soon you'll be able to see your breath when you step outside. The city will put up the big tree downtown. You'll pull out your box of decorations and play music while you wrap lights around the banister. You'll scour thrift stores for the perfect gift. Then you'll wrap up the vintage tour T-shirt and Mariah Carey coffee cup in brown paper. You'll watch your friend's face light up when they unwrap it. You'll eat big meals with people who feel like home. The magnolia trees will hibernate, bloomless and fine with it. You'll remember nothing blooms all year long. Children at the mall will take pictures with Santa, full of nervous energy and hope. You'll remember what it feels like to believe in something.

If it's winter, stick around for spring. Soon it will be warm enough to wear your favorite T-shirt without a jacket covering it up. You won't shiver when you walk the dog. You'll switch from hot coffee to iced. Peanut butter eggs will be back on drugstore shelves and blueberries will be in season. Wildflowers will line the highway with color. The robins will sing love songs for each other, and you'll get to bear witness. Tulips will fill flower beds in grocery store parking lots. The bears and the squirrels and the wood frogs and the groundhogs will come out of hibernation. You'll remember life always begins again. The perennial you thought died in January's ice storm will surprise you with a bloom. You'll remember how much can be survived.

reasons to stick around
for a night

If sticking around for a while is unfathomable, stick around for a night. Stick around to see the sunrise in the morning. Stick around to walk your dog. Stick around to feed your cat. Stick around to get a Twix at the gas station on the way to work and eat it with your lunch. Stick around to listen to your favorite song on your morning commute. Stick around to call your best friend tomorrow and hear how their test went. Stick around to eat pasta or Taco Bell or a pizza for dinner tomorrow. Stick around to see another episode of the series you're watching. Stick around to find out if your favorite contestant makes it to the next episode.

Stick around for whatever mundane reason gets you to your next breath. Stick around for tomorrow so time can show you that you are not as trapped as it feels like you are. Stick around to look back someday and thank yourself for making it to the morning.

on hope springing eternal

Your worst fear might come true. They leave you, they never loved you to start with, they cheat, you cheat, your friend doesn't want to be your friend anymore, you lose your job and have to move back to your hometown with your tail between your legs. Whatever it is, it might be as bad as you thought. Worse, even.

But the next morning when the sun hits your skin, an involuntary shiver of joy will run up your spine like it always does. Your egg sandwich will taste just as good as it did yesterday. Later on, a dog on the subway will lick your shin or a baby will grab your nose or your best friend will say something especially ridiculous. Maybe you won't smile this time. But it will occur to you that you will again, and that will be enough to get you through the week.

Slowly you'll realize that when people say hope springs eternal, they don't really mean it about the springing. They mean it trickles. They mean it limps.

that's cringe

When your eyes cast judgment on someone else's face,
lower them to your chest.
Open the French doors of your rib cage
and whisper to your heart:
What permission has their heart granted them
that you are denying me?

when you're lonely,
ask a stranger for the time

Or tell the woman at the crosswalk that you like her red boots.
If your coworker asks how you're doing, tell the truth. Ask
a passerby for a coffee shop recommendation instead of
asking Google. Crack a little joke to the person next to you
in the elevator. Bring the park security guard a fun fact
every morning.

These are small things. They will not fix you. But once,
at the grocery store, I accidentally patted an old woman's
hand as we reached for the same head of romaine.

I said: *I'm sorry about that! Great minds think alike!*

She replied, *Don't be! That's the only touch I'll get today.*

And I laughed. *Me too.*

the gathering of the graceless

So, you fell from grace.
And not in the delicate, strategic way you planned.

You showed your pain—and no, it wasn't a single tear running
down your cheek in the moonlight from sadness about
something endearing. It was snot-sobs running from your nose
into your mouth.

You showed your rage—not your therapized, articulate, chess-
game rage—but temper-tantrum-on-the-grocery-store-floor-
type rage. It was a shouting match in the movie theater lobby.

You showed your jealousy—they saw you flinch when
they mentioned their other best friend. You showed your
vanity—they caught you checking yourself out in the spoon
on your date. You showed your filth. The screen time.
The cigarettes. The three days without a bath.

So, you got caught. What now? Well, finally! I'm glad
you made it—welcome to the gathering of the graceless.

You can leave your perfection and piety and composure in the
hallway next to your coat. It's warm in here and we made pizzas
and we love you even when you don't have anything nice to say.
Even when you brag. Even when you're jealous. Even when you
kick and scream on the grocery store floor. No matter what
skeletons live in your closet. No matter what skeletons
live in your mind right now.

I have a light if you need one, and a spoon if you want to check yourself out. I brag too, and the skeletons in my closet could use some friends.

a vow to tell them

When their laugh lights up the car. How good they are at fixing things. That I think they're smart enough to be president. How impressive it is that they can answer so many *Jeopardy!* questions. That I think they're funny enough to be on *SNL*. That I love their style, their food, their singing voice, their taste in coffee cups. Every sweet story I can remember about us. That I'm honored when people say we look alike. That they are the mother, father, sister, aunt, cousin, partner, friend of my dreams. The nice things I say behind their back. That I hope they live in peace. That I hope they live in power. A vow to deliver a thousand eulogies for every person I love. While we all go on living, while we all still can hear.

the tune of tomorrow

The key to sticking around is a breakfast sandwich waiting for you at the café that opens at 8 A.M. The key to sticking around is picturing your dog's next birthday. The key to sticking around is planning your Halloween costume even if it's July. The key to sticking around is lying on the warm pavement in your driveway and noticing how it feels just like it did when you were a kid. The key to sticking around is ordering a new shirt and choosing the slowest shipping option.

On your darkest nights, when next year feels unfathomable and you're tempted to stop the music—

Could you just sing me the tune of tomorrow?

life finds a way

You wake up wishing you were dead, and then get out of bed to walk the dog.

Outside, Main Street smells like shit warmed up. Down the block, sullen teenagers holding musical instruments trickle into the performing arts school. A poster taped to the window of one of the classrooms has smiling cartoon flowers on it and reads GROW THROUGH WHAT YOU GO THROUGH. When you walk past it, you scoff so loudly your dog jumps.

And yet, summer is passing one godforsaken day at a time, and you *are* growing through what you went through. It isn't pretty. But you force your life through the sidewalk cracks anyway. You reach down to your roots looking for the gumption to put yourself out of your misery, and instead you find a frustratingly unkillable will to live, no matter the stink of the street.

You're growing through what you went through. Not like a flower. Like a weed.

joy as a stray cat
and forgotten song

You haven't forgotten how to love your life. Even if you don't remember the sound of your real laugh, and all you want is to be left alone, or you can't remember the last time you had a dream (though all you do is sleep), I promise—you haven't forgotten how to love your life.

Think of it like this: Joy is a stray. She won't let you put a collar on her, and she doesn't come when she's called, but she's never far. She's easy to lose and hard to kill.

Or do you remember that day we walked around for hours, lost as butterflies on the seafloor, until we spotted the pizza place we went to that one time—and suddenly we knew exactly how to get home? Do you remember how on our way back, we passed that man playing piano on Texas Street? How you couldn't remember the name of the song to save your life, but you sang every word?

loved until proven otherwise

Growing up, my mother was always chatting up somebody:
the fast-food cashier, the customer service representative,
whoever was behind her in line at Ross or Dollar General.
Mortified preteen me would try to hurry her along,
asking, *What if they don't want to talk to you?*
She would always say the same thing in response:
I guess I'm a pig with perfume under my nose.

I never asked what she meant, but I think I know now.
Let me assume sweetness of this world and its opinions of me.
When life puts an apple in my mouth, let me take it for a snack.
Let me use one of my ears to make a silk purse
while I listen for blessings with the other.

for the ones who left

There's a corner of the universe where you stayed. In the lukewarm relationship. At the good-on-paper, bad-on-your-soul job. In the town that felt like fourth-grade shoes on fifth-grade feet.

You're happy there, maybe. Happy enough. You have nice wineglasses, and candles you can afford to burn daily, and a love that feels like enough—if you don't think about it too hard.

On nights like this, you pour your nice wine into your nice wineglass and light your nice candle and it's a nice life. But every now and then, a shiver of something primal and indomitable runs up your spine. Every now and then you lurch awake in the middle of the night, gasping for air.

As if you were just running.

for the ones who stayed

Sometimes, metamorphosis starts with a bang. Just like in the movies: *Girl is miserable. Girl abruptly abandons everything she knows to go on a far-flung adventure. Girl finds herself along the way.*

But sometimes it starts with a whisper. Maybe you don't need to quit your job or leave your partner or buy a Sprinter van. Maybe you can grow wings right where you are. Maybe today, that looks like mustering the courage to correct someone who mispronounces your name. Or going to your small-town Walgreens in a Lower East Side outfit. Or stepping into the pottery studio you've walked past a hundred times. Maybe your unfurling will be imperceptible to anyone but you.

We forget:

From outside the cocoon, it looks like nothing is happening.

the woman you hate

I try to support all women, but some women make it hard.
When I spot that one girl in a photo, the love and light
drain out of my body.

I can't help but think:

What does anyone see in her?
She's attention seeking.
She's not nearly as smart as she thinks she is.
She's not a good person.
And I hate to be an asshole, but her teeth aggravate me.

Then I take a deep breath and say:

I do not speak about myself that way anymore.

it's your party,
cry if you want to

Don't put all your eggs in one basket.
Don't make a mountain out of a molehill.
Don't cry over spilled milk.

But maybe you know which basket you want.
Maybe it's no one's place to tell you what's a molehill.
Maybe crying over spilled milk is better than feeling **nothing**.

In a land of
don't, don't, don't
I hope you do.

in defense of flying
too close to the sun

Curiosity killed the cat
and hurled Icarus into the sea.

Or was it hope?
I think that might be what we're here to do—
strap beeswax wings onto our breakable bodies,
knowing how it could end, and
fly toward the light of life anyway.

shoot your shit-shot

Hope is a shit-shoot.

Hope tells you to apply for your dream school—test scores be damned! Then when the response comes in a standard letter-size envelope and not a big, promising packet—hope stares at you blankly and shrugs. Hope screams at you to ask out the person you like. Then when you get rejected, hope offers you a stupid platitude about shooting for the moon. Hope tells you tomorrow will be better, and it isn't. And then tomorrow hope tells you the next day will be better, and it isn't. And the next day—I think you can guess what happens.

Hope is a shit-shoot.
And you know what else?
Hope is the only thing worth anything.

Hope is the wind in your sails as you approach the person who will become your everything. Hope is the postage stamp on questions that render the most important yeses you'll ever hear. Hope is what gets you out of places you don't fit anymore. Hope is the only path toward the tomorrow that *will be better*.

Hope is a shit-shoot.
A shit-shot worth taking.
The only shot we have.

a time for everything

Once, I was running late walking to work
when a parade of thousands of bicycles
barreled onto the street I was waiting to cross.
I don't know whether to laugh or to cry,
I said to the coworker I called,
explaining why I'd be even later than I thought.
A man sitting on the sidewalk behind me said,
Laugh!

whose hate did you swallow?

Eventually the mean voice in your head will come
knocking again. The one that shouts sermons about
your inadequacy.

When it does, let it in.

Hang its coat on the hook and give it a cup of tea.
Pay attention when it speaks and notice the lilt of its vowels.
Something is curious about the way it pronounces its *T*'s . . .

Listen closely and maybe you'll realize—*it isn't your voice.*

this is why I don't get
my hopes up

you say, with hope spilled all in the dirt.
This is why I don't trust anyone, you say,
through tears that betray your words.
I need to get a hold of myself, you say,
but I hope that you never do.
Don't get me wrong, I know it hurts,
but this is what I hope for you:

May your spirit never be broken
by something as common as sense.
When they say not to look the pasture horse in the mouth,
may you break into a gallop and jump its fence.
May fear throw its lasso a thousand times
only to find your soul is something it just can't catch.
May your heart sprint like hell every chance that it gets,
headed for the coop, to count the chickens before they hatch.

ready, set, don't go

Ten years from now, it's a spring Saturday morning in 2035.
You're standing in the yard of the house you bought in 2034.
Humming a song from a 2033 album by your favorite band,
who you found out about in 2032. Waiting for the dog you
got in 2031 to finish doing their business. Wearing your
comfiest pajama pants: a birthday gift you received in 2030
from a friend you met in 2029. You're planning to spend
the afternoon gardening, a hobby you picked up in 2028.
Later, you might rewatch a movie you love, the one that
won Best Picture in 2027. Inside, someone you met in 2026
is making pancakes.

All because your world didn't end in 2025.

my body's keeper

Today I resent my responsibility
to keep this needy, bloody, selfish
creature of a body alive.
But, I will set it in the sun
and brush its hair.
I will bathe it
and tuck covers under its neck.
I will feed it bread
and hold water to its lips.
I will pretend it's a dog
or a friend, something I love.
I will hope for the best.

I have learned to love things before.

IV.

A World Where Love
Calls the Shots

Out beyond ideas of wrongdoing and rightdoing,
There is a field. I'll meet you there.

—Rumi

airborne

Today you said you wanted to take me
to the pool where you went swimming
growing up, once it's warm enough.
And my heart's tail started thumping,
thinking of you thinking of us
a whole season from now.

When I was little, I loved swimming too,
but I loved the diving boards more.
I'd stand in the dripping line waiting
to try the same flip again and again.
I'd belly flop the landing
and get right back in line.

This could all go wrong, of course.
But I'll risk a sucker punch
waiting in the water for the moment
after the jump and before the smack.
Heels over head and heart midflip.
This might hurt like hell in a second
but right now, I'm airborne.
And you never know,
this could be the first time
I land feetfirst.

for your cold, dead heart

Another failed love.
I must have a cold, dead heart, you say.
I blink at you.

A cold, dead heart wouldn't choose the misshapen potatoes at the farmer's market so they aren't picked last. Someone with a cold, dead heart wouldn't usher a soaked passerby under their umbrella. They wouldn't buy a slice of cake for the crying stranger at the airport. They wouldn't ask questions about the baby pictures in a stranger's wallet.

Your heart remembers birthdays and phone numbers and favorite colors of the hearts that left. Your heart may be black and blue.

But it's still leaping out of your chest.

don't bite the hand
that helps you

I'm wrestling my latest craigslist find—a large orange
velvet chair—toward my front door when my neighbor
shouts at me from her porch.

Can I help you with that?

I've never known how to act around helping hands.
I avoid them like the plague.

Thanks, but I've got it.

My neighbor laughs.

I know you do. But that looks heavy!

There's an idea: to accept help—not because I can't
carry it alone, but simply because it's heavy.

high-school best friend

Would 8 Eastern work for our call?
How about 7? Let me know how
the meeting went. Could you send
me your new address one more time?
I sent you a little stupid thing.
Happy Thanksgiving, love you!
Merry Christmas, love you!
Love you! I love you! I love you.
I meant to tell you: The other day
I got lost with a dead phone and
borrowed a stranger's to call
someone to come get me. But
then I realized, the only number
I know by heart is yours.

blindside

Before I take my dog to the vet,
I always say sorry in a particular way.
I draw out the vowels, low and slow.
I chew the word the same every time.
By now, she knows what it means
and starts slinking around sadly
before we even leave the house.

That's by design.
I figure, the golden rule and all that.
If you're going to hurt me,
I'd like a heads-up.
Better that than me thinking
I'm on the way to the park
wagging my tail like an idiot
until you stop the car
and we aren't where I thought we were going
and you're telling me this is for my own good
while you're walking away,
and my stupid heart is still beating fast
from what it thought was a thrill.

how to trust again

Notice how knots form in your stomach when you think about getting back out there. Say yes anyway. Put on a good song while the bath gets hot. Scrub off as many old stories about yourself as you can. Step onto your bath mat and spritz yourself with Tom Ford's Fucking Fabulous. Dress in whatever makes you believe it. Have a glass of red while you wait. When the doorbell rings, give your racing heart a pep talk. Say: *You do not have to be still. Your fear makes perfect sense.* Then swing the door wide open with shaking hands, and invite possibility inside.

against soulmates

You ask if I think we were written in the stars.
I tap a finger to my lips.
Have you heard of desire paths? I ask.

You'd know one if you saw it. They're the dirt paths that veer
away from the asphalt in places where there isn't a path, but
there should be. They're created not with concrete or machinery
or urban planning committees, but with feet—thousands of
defiant feet that said, *There should be a path here,* and trod
one into place.

When god made our souls, I don't think she made a path
between them. I don't think a supernova blasted a line between
you and me. But the first time I saw you, I thought, *There
should be a path here,* and so we made one. By walking to each
other's apartments. Stepping nervously into Upper West Side
restaurants. Walking through the door of your mom's house,
then mine. Trudging into the grocery store mad as hell, and
strolling out hand in hand. Leaving. Coming back.

We made this.
The stars don't deserve the credit.

the finer things

Do you promise me we'll reach for a top-shelf life?
I want something better than premium economy,
more than a one-Michelin-star dinner,
bigger than the junior suite at the W Hotel.

Do you promise me we'll reach for the *really* good stuff?
Like the finest Chardonnay available
at the 7-Eleven, on the way to the beach.
Like a tent, two sleeping bags, and
galaxies of non-Michelin stars.
Like driving instead of flying,
with the radio blasting and the windows down.
Like sharing a sandwich at the top of the hike
and wondering how we got so well-off.

for arguments
with someone you love

Like every storm, it starts with one stupid drop. An overflowing garbage can. A bad joke. Your sneakers on the white couch, which you know I hate.

Then cloud nine evaporates and tenderness gets thrown to the wind. My tongue spits lightning that rattles our apartment and your eyes roll back thunder that scares the dog.

But even under our darkest skies, the sweet gleam in your eye always catches the light. And as soon as it does, I remember—you're cold and wet too.

What do you say we skip to after the storm? I'll bottle my lightning if you patch up our cloud's silver lining. Let's jump to clear skies. Petrichor. Glossy pavement. You and me, hand-in-hand on the porch, assessing the damage. A few trees down. Some shingles missing from the roof. Nothing we can't fix.

All things considered, right as rain.

after you take off
the purity ring

Try to forget the lesson of the raggedy rose, ruined by being
passed around a crowd. The old tape, stuck on too many things
to be sticky anymore. The chewed gum. Squeezed toothpaste.
Dirty water. Remember: You are a person, not an object.

Invite lust over for dinner. Eat with your hands. When a
chapter of your book turns you on, read it again. Share old,
sad stories with friends. They will become hilarious. Tell how
you got caught with the teddy bear. Hear how they got caught
with the chair leg, the faucet, the hairbrush handle. Watch
how shame evaporates when you hold it up to the light.

When you're ready, step up to the plate. Resolve to play
your own game. Remember: Sometimes, true love waits.
Other times, it heads right up to bat. Lets out a victory whoop
as it slides into home in the first inning.

this or that

They say bisexuals are greedy, and they're right if they're talking about me.

My elementary-school breakfast was five fried eggs, and most mornings, I'd board the bus wishing I'd had a sixth. On fried chicken day in the cafeteria, my classmates would trade legs for wings, wings for breasts. I held my tray close to my chest, wary of giving up any pieces. I liked them all.

For years I prayed the hunger away. I brought God pieces of myself I didn't want, like a pawn shop. *If I don't think that way for a whole month, will you take it?* He never bid.

Spend enough time with a growling stomach and you become a bottomless pit. It is what it is—I want it both ways. I want heads, tails, and the beveled edge in between. I want shotgun and I want to drive. I want your love any way it's served. I want to eat it with my hands. I want to lick my fingers. I want the left side of the menu and the right. I want to bat my eyelashes while I joke with the waitress.

I'll have one of everything, please.

the fig you've chosen

After Sylvia Plath

Somewhere in the fig tree of choices, I have four daughters.
I braid their hair. Write *I love you* on ziplocked sandwiches.
Push tiny fingers into tiny mittens. I shiver, tethered to
a suburban porch as they step onto the bus. I love them so
much it makes my mouth dry. When I look in the bathroom
mirror and don't see myself in it, I look away.

On a different branch, I am as slippery as an eel. Solitary as
a subway train. I am a master of the art of nursing a cocktail.
Hailing a cab. Leaving before I'm left. My pointy shoes tap
out an endless cadence in bustling lobbies and pristine offices
on Central Park West. I know their rhythm by heart and most
nights I like the sound of it. And on the second Sunday in May,
when I see tiny hands clutching ziplocked sandwiches on the
B train, I look away.

In the palm of my hand is the fig I picked: you and me. This.
We live in a city that feels like a suburb, our compromise
between tethered and slippery. There's a sprawling mall where
I inspect pairs of tiny mittens and pointy shoes carefully, as if
I have a purpose for them, and then walk away. It's me making
coffee and you eating a banana and me telling you, *I love you,
I love our life.*

And I do. I really do.

you don't have to label yourself

If the shoe fits, wear it. If it doesn't, frolic barefoot in the field
past language. Head out to where you keep things you don't
have words to describe. Like how you felt the first time you
saw a newborn. Why you remember places you've never been.
The color of your best friend's hair, like embers mixed with
sunshine mixed with . . . something. Why sun-showers make
you cry. Your location that time you lay on the line between
North and South Carolina—there wasn't a name for it,
but for once, you knew exactly where you were.

same love, different languages

I say, *I think we find each other in every life.*

You say, *I got us groceries.*

I say, *Our souls must have been part of the same star billions of years ago.*

You say, *It seems like you liked those sparkling waters so I got more.*

I say, *I wrote you a love poem today but I'm not ready to read it to you yet.*

You say, *Don't forget your property taxes are due January 31.*

I say, *Actually, I am ready, I'll go get it. But you can't laugh.*

You say, *I won't laugh.*

And you don't. You never do.
You listen so closely,
I almost believe you like poems.

object permanence

So are you straight now?
My phone lights up with questions I wish no one asked.
Breaking news: *WOMAN TAKEN FOR STRAIGHT WHEN
DATING A MAN AND GAY WHEN DATING A WOMAN.*
Tale as old and tired as time.

I look through my window at the Moon and consider
all the names we call her. Crescent, full, gibbous, new,
each one deemed just a phase. How human of us
to trace her silhouette in relation to our own.

Meanwhile, the Moon sits two hundred thousand miles
away in silence, as she did for eons before us. Neither
waning nor waxing, never anything but whole.
Perhaps she's charmed by our naïveté. Look at the
humans playing peekaboo. Covering their eyes
with their hands, slowly realizing that
what they can't see is still there.

creation myth

On one hand, I believe the no-nonsense telling
of how we got here. The single cell that multiplied,
the fish that grew legs and crawled to land, the apes
that started to walk upright. Some days, I think
that is all there was to it. A big bang and dumb luck.

And yet: You looked so angelic that first morning,
I found myself thinking that the bridge of your nose
must have been sculpted by careful, divine fingertips.
That surely your lips were etched onto your face by
something that loves you. That only a holy mind
could have come up with an idea as good as us.

ode to trans bravery

I see you.
You, killer of the name that never suited your soul.
You, standing on the shoulders of a muted legacy.
You, shouting for everyone who couldn't and can't.
You, walking through fire while you blaze a trail.
You, writing love letters to the future with history's pen.

You, fearfully and wonderfully made,
fearfully and wonderfully in the making.

things I don't say to strangers I used to know

I know we're strangers now, but I still peel mangoes
using the rim of a glass like you taught me. I still get
the Number 6, no egg, at the Thai place on Franklin.
But I eat both spring rolls now.

I can still hear your voice telling me that a person
doesn't really die until they're thought about
for the last time. I still feel bad for making you cry
in the grocery store parking lot about my off-brand
Cheerios. I still worry about your brother. I still do
my eyeliner the way you showed me. And I still hope
you slow down on the highway. Maybe you do now.

I know we're strangers now but if I ever hear you're
in Houston, I'll buy real Cheerios, just in case. I know
we're strangers now but if you die before I do,
I'll keep you alive.

for the one you don't know how to help

I don't know the way out of your woods, but I'll stay with you in the neck of them. And I know happiness doesn't grow on trees, but I'd bark up the wrong one with you any day.

You are not out of the woods, and I don't know how to fix your pain. I have nothing to offer you, but I promise you this—when a tree falls in your forest, it will always make a sound.

Because I will always be there to hear it.

I have bad news and good news

If you aren't cool enough for them now / the eight-hundred-dollar coat won't help / You can move to a cooler part of town / they still won't want to come over / Waiting to reply until tomorrow / won't make them text you back sooner / You can learn how to say *Cannes* and *Houston Street* and *açaí* / they will find other reasons to judge you / When you work hard on your makeup for dinner / they'll ask: *Why are you so dressed up* / If you aren't enough for them now / you never will be

But

there are people who / aren't daunted by the commute to your place / don't care how much your coat costs / won't bump you behind them when the street is too narrow for three / think you're beautiful when you're dressed to the nines / and when you're dressed to the ones / won't be scared away by your dark past / or your bad temper / or your worst mistakes / let alone by three messages in a row / When you find the right people / and you will find them / you can have nothing / and it will be plenty

god (any pronouns)

I asked god, *What do you like to be called?*
She said, *I have too many names to keep up.*

I pressed. *Be honest: Do you mind the lowercase G?*
God yawned. *I've got bigger fish to fry than capitalization.*

I wanted a commandment.
Can you at least tell me your pronouns?
They just laughed.
Honey, you can try to put the stars in a bucket any way you like.

So I call god a new name every day. Holy mother, holy father,
and holy parent. Dogwood tree, blue jay, and Terlingua sky.
The beginning, the end, and the middle. He answers to it all.

I think of her when I see RuPaul on TV responding to questions
about pronouns: *You can call me he. You can call me she. You
can call me Regis and Kathie Lee. I don't care!*

Just as long as you call me.

group text

Did we decide on a time for tomorrow / Where should we meet / I can bring that bottle of wine we didn't drink last week / Stop apologizing / You are not bragging / You never cease to amaze me / I'm infuriated for you / You are not dumb / I would have thought the same thing / He needs to pull his shit together / How did it go / Glad you're feeling better / Can we have a group cry this weekend / We might have to be on the lawn to get four spots together / I'm so excited I could die / Fuck their engagement / I don't care if she's Mother Teresa / You do not look raggedy / You do not look haggard / You do not look like hot garbage / You do not look like The Rock / You are not a bad person / You are the furthest thing from lazy / You are not peaking / This is just the beginning / This is so you / So us / ETA 5:03 / We're in the back / Do you see me / I'm waving / I see you

playing god

If god has a plan, I don't think they're fussy about it. Maybe god thinks about their plan the way your grandma thought about your birthday. She used to get you an American Girl doll every year, but once she realized you didn't like them, she swapped them for Power Rangers.

Maybe god writes in pencil. Maybe your words are holy too. Maybe god delights in edits. Maybe there's no such thing as *assigned at birth*. Maybe god doesn't assign anything—they just start the conversation.

Maybe god says:

For I know the plans I have for you.
But if you have something else in mind,
just say the Word.

V.

A World Where Heaven Happens Now

I don't know what God is.
I don't know what death is.

But I believe they have between them
     some fervent and necessary arrangement.

     —Mary Oliver

wet, hot heart

Ashes to ashes, dust to dust, but
so much happens in between.
I was ashes and then
I had a wet, hot heart.
I was dust and then
I was taking a bath, I was
burning my knuckle on the grill,
I was in the pool with my friend.
Soon enough I'll be dust again,
I'll be drier than bone and back
where I came from. Soon
I'll be scattered in the wind, but for now,
I'll get out of bed. Sloppily kiss
my dog good morning, open the curtains,
and have my hot drink. Use my wet breath
to hum a living song.

pando aspen grove

You're living your life, and I'm living mine.
I've never been to the places you frequent.
You've never met the people I love.
We're two parallel lines with our own
daily routines and aches and pains.

Let's say we beat the odds and cross paths—
our towels are spread out on the same beach,
my car is next to yours on the highway,
your table is next to mine at the diner—
still, we're nothing to each other.

Almost everyone is a stranger until you zoom in or pan out.
At the beach, we might keep a polite distance in the water
but if you ask the birds, we're two side-by-side dots.
On the highway, we'd stay in our lanes—but if we crashed,
your insides would look just like mine on the autopsy table.
At the diner, maybe we wouldn't make eye contact, and would
leave with no idea we're both from Enola, Pennsylvania:
alone spelled backwards.

Recently someone told me about a forest in Utah
where all the trees share a single set of roots.
The trunks in the East will never touch the ones in the West,
and the leaves in the front are oblivious to the ones in the back
and yet—at the source, the forest is all one tree.

you can work
when you're dead

Well, no, you can't. But what I mean is: Rest your head on your lover's chest for a few more minutes. Clock in late. Take the long way home that passes by the horses, even when your inbox is tapping your shoulder. Close your laptop on the plane and look at the clouds. When you can't find time to read or do yoga or play your ukulele, look again. Send the call to voicemail. Go to a coffee shop to work with a friend. Talk about everything except work. Decline the meeting invite. Take a day to drive eighty miles to get your favorite dim sum. Turn your camera off during the Zoom call and bake a strawberry shortcake while the CEO waxes on about revenue.

I have so much to do, you always say.
But the doing always gets done.
It's the living you should keep an eye on.

lost and found

When I lose my faith in humanity, I go to the beach. Any shitty beach will do. Today, a sun-licked couple headed to their car hastens to a trot when they see me scanning for spots. Past the dunes, a mother lets her son bury her in the mealy sand, smiling like she loves shells in her nooks and crannies. A family pulls wet Coronas from a Styrofoam cooler, music wafting from their speaker, softening the silence between people who know everything and nothing about each other.

On the shore, a leathery man rubs a metal detector over the low tide line. When I ask him if he is looking for anything in particular, he shakes his head.

Even when it beeps, it's usually trash.
But once, I found a 14-karat bracelet, so I keep the faith.

I walk away, wheels turning. There's an idea: A faith you don't have to find. A faith you can just keep.

what heaven smells like

your aunt's perfume / public library books / movie theater
butter / the first snow of the year / blown-out birthday candles /
the woods behind your house / pool chlorine / the vanilla-bean
lotion you loved in sixth grade / peach snow-cone syrup / your
grandma's house / cinnamon-sugar toast / road trip gasoline /
sweet potato casserole / a damp nylon tent after the rain / state
fair funnel cake / every person you've ever loved / your dad's
breath / like coffee mixed with mouthwash / your dog's paws /
like corn chips and grass / your lover's slept-on pillow /
fresh from a dream / that felt like a life

you're going to die, so live

Which is to say, give time a hell of a battle
even though you know you'll lose the war.
Wrestle every second of sunlight
and laughter and French-kissing
that you can from regret's hands.
Snatch hours of tenderness
from the jaws of apathy.
Yank daydreams and poems
from boredom's scalp.
When nihilism swings at you,
swing back. Hiss through clenched teeth:
I may not live forever,
but goddamnit, I am alive today.

miracles

They don't make them like they used to.
Well, except at Newport Beach, where the water
glows in the dark. And murmurations, the way
thousands of starlings move as one, like a wave.
Oh, and have you ever been to Eternal Flame Falls?
There's a nook in the waterfall with a little flame
that never goes out.

Of course, everything has an explanation these days.
Bioluminescent algae, natural gas seeps, all that.
And I read that sometimes the wind actually *does*
blow out the flame, and hikers relight it.

So, if *miracle* isn't the word you'd use to describe
thousands of human hands moving as one—
like a beating heart—to guard a flame
that has nothing to offer them, then
what would you call it?

what's the meaning of life?

Can we talk about that tomorrow? Tonight, let's dance till the
sun comes up. Or on second thought, maybe Wednesday
morning? It's going to be too nice tomorrow not to go to the
beach. Wait, could we actually touch base next week? I told my
best friend I'd get bagels with her that day. And honestly, I don't
want to waste your time—I'm not sure what life means. Your
guess is as good as mine. All I know is that the living part seems
important. The sun and salt and bread of it all. They say woman
can't live on bread alone, but I think bread seems like a good
place to start.

death as a surprise party

You fumble for your keys at the front door.
Your tired feet shuffle through the dark hallway.
You turn on the kitchen light and can't believe your eyes.

Maybe you see a room full of people you love, each beaming.
But maybe what happens next is harder to explain than that.
One of those wonderful *you had to be there* moments.

In any event, you're glad you didn't know what was coming—
it would have ruined the surprise.

god on main street

What did you say? *Do I know God?*
Yeah! Are you looking for her?
I'd check Main Street,
she sits there with a shopping cart sometimes.
She's the sweetest. She calls my dog *princess*.

Yesterday, I saw her two blocks over
sprouted in a crack in the sidewalk.
That must have been her, right?
Only God could bloom in concrete.

I ate lunch with her last week and
at first, I didn't recognize her.
But she's always the one person
who never looks away from you
even when the story you're telling
gets long and boring and confusing.

I saw her waitressing last Wednesday.
And a few days before that, I saw her making
shoes out of trash for some barefoot guy.
She's always doing stuff like that.

Anyway, good luck! You'll find her soon,
she doesn't go far.

it's either gorgeous
or devastating

The care we pour into temporary things. Like how we know
birthday cards all end up in landfills, but still dig for the perfect
words to write in them. The way we draw hearts on fogged-up
windshields, even though we know they'll disappear in a breath.
How we know we won't live in our houses forever, but we still
paint the walls and mark the doorways with our children's
heights and bury our dogs in the backyard.

Let's go with *gorgeous*. Gorgeous, radiantly reckless, and brave:
to know your world is made of sand and still try to build a
castle. To carry on as the tide approaches. To allow yourself
to hunt for treasure in what's slipping through your fingers.

death as jumping
off the high dive

I hope death feels like summer, like the first jump off the high
dive. Goosebumps bloom on your arms as you wait in line—it's
barely June, and the sun is almost down. You watch one friend
jump, and then another, and then it's your turn.

Your stomach flips as you climb the ladder. You step onto the
board and cling on to the metal rails. From here, you can see
the cars in the parking lot and the road that brought you
here—it all looks so small.

From the shallow end of the pool, your dad notices you
lingering in the in-between and shouts your name.
I'll count you down, he hollers.

Three . . . You inch your toes to the edge of the board.

Two . . . It's so quiet up here.

One! You jump.

There's a momentary Milky Way of color and euphoria. A sharp
inhale. An enveloping, and then a dissipation of all fear.
Oh yeah, you remember from below the surface.

I've done this before.

god winks

The smell of baby skin, all powder and milk and possibility.
How our veins look like roots and our neurons look like
galaxies. The way water glitters. Dappled light on forest
floors. The wildflowers on the side of U.S. 281. A 7 A.M. call
from your grandma that woke you up just in time for a cotton-
candy sunrise. Eleven consecutive green lights on the way to
the hospital.

Whatever makes you think:
If god doesn't love me,
she *sure* is leading me on.

the view from the bottom
of the hill we're dying on

They say we're killing the Earth, but it's *us* we'll kill in the end.
Earth watched the dinosaurs come and go without breaking a
sweat. She took an asteroid to the face and kept her chin up.
She was here when we came and she'll be here when we're gone.

Once our lease runs out and we're finished warming
and bombing ourselves to death,
Earth will tie up her hair and get to work.

Balsam trees will burst through empty highways
while ivy hurries to hide billboards.
Gale-force winds will uproot building foundations.
Skyscrapers will slump and then fall,
and the dirt underneath will sigh with relief.

Earth will click her tongue while she works.
Those humans didn't stay very long,
but they sure did make a mess.

let me let you go

There's a phrase Southern women say when they're on the phone: *Let me let you go.* The subtext is: *Well, I won't hold you up any longer.* The subtext of the subtext is: *I need to get off the phone.*

(Invariably, the call lasts at least fifteen more minutes.)

Growing up, I never understood the tap dance of the *let me let you go*s. Why do we say we need to go, only to keep talking?

Now, I know those delays are prayers. This life only lasts for a moment. I see no better reason to linger than to cling to holy, mundane togetherness as it slips through our hands.

God, grant me the courage to hold on for dear life to things I know I will lose. God, let me keep the people I love on the line for as many fifteen-more-minutes as I can.

Only when I have to, God, let me let them go.

don't save joy for last

If I spent less time sitting in the sun and more time sitting
at my desk, maybe I could really make something of myself.

If I read fewer romance novels and more self-help books,
maybe I could find the formula to unlock the life of my dreams.

If I spent less money on lavender lattes and put more money in
the bank, maybe someday I could afford a big house,
with a wraparound porch.

Where I could sit in the sun. Read a romance novel.
Have a lavender latte.

some things you have
to decide for yourself

Eve's questions tumbled out
between bites of forbidden fruit.

Am I good?
The tree of knowledge answered *YES.*

Am I evil?
The tree of knowledge answered *YES.*

Which one am I mostly?
The tree of knowledge was silent.

after the ball drops

It's New Year's Eve, the biggest party night of the year. Naturally, I'm in bed watching a documentary about wood frogs.

The wood frog, I am learning, is a tiny master of survival. Each year, to survive the harsh Alaskan winter, they freeze solid for several months. As temperatures drop, ice takes over the wood frog's body, freezing its veins and turning its eyes glassy white. For months, the wood frog is a wood frog popsicle: hard as a rock, heartbeatless, brain-dead, and yet—alive. Winter ends eventually, and the wood frogs begin to thaw out. First, their heartbeats return. Then, brain activity. And then, the crescendo: They start to move, take a gulp of fresh air, and then they hop.

Like most things, the wood frogs remind me of you. How you too are a tiny master of survival. I think about when you used to buy an advent calendar whenever you needed a daily reason not to kick your own bucket. You may not know how to freeze your blood, but find me a frog that has valued its life less than a Lindt truffle—and lived to tell the tale.

How ubiquitous it is, the dirty work of surviving. Every critter and creature sings the same fight and flight song. We look for gods and palm miniature jam jars and light joints and read holy books and have sex and grow exoskeletons and freeze our blood, and it's all more or less the same thing. A frenetic battening of eroding hatches.

The documentary says scientists can't explain what starts the wood frog's heart again after being frozen and lifeless all winter. I imagine the wood frogs can't explain either. Survival's funny like that: After months with no pulse and out of the blue, your heart starts to beat again. You notice it's spring. You hop toward the water, to look for love.

death as the morning
after a sleepover

I hope death feels like the morning after a sleepover. Your best friend's front door swings open to reveal your mom on the porch, silhouetted by the July sun. You know the answer but you ask anyway. *Can I stay a little longer?*

Behind her, the car engine hums knowingly and your dog peeks out of the back-seat window. *I'm so glad you had fun, baby, but it's time to go home.*

She reaches across the threshold for your hand. You take hers, then look back one more time.

Thank you for having me.

map says you are here

I went looking where they said heaven is
but I must have taken a wrong turn.
I couldn't find the throne.
I didn't hear the choir.
No one I love was there.
So, I came back down to Earth,
wet from the clouds.
Nothing to show for all my effort.
I walked in the house,
head drooped with defeat.
I sat in my dad's chair,
still warm from the ball game.
My mom was making fried bologna
like her mom used to.
My niece was singing her show songs
and it sounded a little
holy. I cocked my head to the side,
looked at the map.
Could this be what they meant?
They said on Earth, as it is in heaven.
They said on Earth.

the last day of my life

On the last day of my life, I hope I'm tired.
Not tired like after a bad night of sleep,
tired like after a really good trip.
Tired from museum mornings and sightseeing afternoons,
tired from not wasting a moment.

On the last day of my life, I hope my body is worn out.
Not worn out like something that wasn't taken care of,
worn out like something that was well used.
Worn out with laugh lines and ink under my skin,
worn out from decades of sunny summers and wedding cakes.
Worn out with love.

On the last day of my life, I hope I'm ready.
Not ready like ready to leave somewhere,
ready like ready to *go* somewhere.
Ready to get back,
ready to see my mom and my dog.
Ready to fade into the static that made me.

Don't get me wrong, I love a good trip.
I hope I have a really good time.
But the best part of a trip is
coming home.

Acknowledgments

Thanks to you, reader, for spending some of your precious time with this book. Thank you to my online community for making its existence possible. I am still stunned that you listened when I shouted into the void.

Thank you to my literary agent, Steve Harris, for your expertise, advocacy, and big kindness. Thank you to Brianna Pastor for helping me find my way in the publishing world when you had no reason to help me, beyond the sweetness of your heart.

Thank you to the Random House and Convergent teams for giving me a chance. Thank you to Rachel Tockstein, Jessalyn Foggy, Hope Hathcock, Alisse Goldsmith-Wissman, Sarah Horgan, and Cara DuBois for your valuable time and expertise. The biggest thank you to my brilliant editor, Leita Williams. Without you, these poems would be half-baked shells of themselves.

Thank you to my friends: Sarah, Kelly, Amy, Dina, Rachel, and others. Every poem I write about friendship is about you. Thank you to my family. To my legion of aunts, uncles, and cousins: Your voices are the soundtrack of my happiest memories. To my big sister, Kathryn: In my eyes, you can do no wrong. To my dad, who has taught me tons about love without ever having to say a word about it. To my mom, who will always be my blueprint. Thank you to the love of my life and my favorite person on the planet, Roy. Nothing else matters as long as you're in my corner, and you always are.

© NATALIE GAYNOR

VICTORIA HUTCHINS is passionate about poetry, mindfulness, and movement. In 2023, she left her career as a corporate attorney to seek a creativity-driven life. *Make Believe* is her first book.

Instagram: @thedailyvictorian
TikTok: @thedailyvictorian

About the Type

This book was set in Minion, a 1990 Adobe Originals typeface by Robert Slimbach. Minion is inspired by classical, old-style typefaces of the late Renaissance, a period of elegant and beautiful type designs. Created primarily for text setting, Minion combines the aesthetic and functional qualities that make text type highly readable with the versatility of digital technology.